little Miss Busy

by Roger Hargreaves

WORLD INTERNATIONAL

Little Miss Busy loved nothing more than to be hard at work, keeping herself busy.

As busy as a bee.

In fact, as busy as a hive of bees.

Every day she would get up at three o'clock in the morning.

Then, Little Miss Busy,
would read a chapter from her favourite book.

It was called:
"Work is Good for You".

And then she would get down to the housework.

She would begin by tidying up,
and then sweeping,
and dusting,
and scrubbing,
and polishing,
until everything was spotless.

She would clean her house from top to bottom
and then from bottom to top, just to make sure.

She even dusted the bread and polished the butter.

She wasn't happy unless she was busy working.

And she didn't rest all day long, not for a minute,
not even for a second.

From three o'clock in the morning
until after midnight.

That was until last Monday.

Little Miss Busy wasn't up at three o'clock.

She wasn't up by six o'clock.

She wasn't even out of bed by nine o'clock.

She was ill.

"Oh, calamity!" she cried.

"I won't be able to do any work!"

She telephoned Doctor Make-you-well.

Five minutes later he was at her bedside.

He asked her to put out her tongue.

He examined her throat.

And he looked at her hands and feet.

"What you need is rest, a lot of rest,"
he said, with a broad smile.

"A lot of rest," repeated Little Miss Busy to herself.

"Oh, calamity!"

There was a loud THUMP!

Which was the sound of Little Miss Busy
falling over backwards,
on to the bed,
luckily for her.

On Tuesday, Mr Strong
called to see Little Miss Busy.

He brought her 72 eggs.

Go on, count them.

"There is nothing like eggs
for giving you strength," said Mr Strong.

By the seventy-second egg,
Little Miss Busy was feeling much better.

That was, until Mr Strong said,
"Now you must rest to get your strength up."

There was a loud THUMP!

Which was the sound of Little Miss Busy
falling over backwards,
on to the bed,
luckily for her.

On Wednesday, Mr Greedy
came to visit.

He brought an enormous bowl of food.

"I always find that eating a big meal
makes me feel better," said Mr Greedy.

Little Miss Busy ate the lot.

She felt better than ever.

That was until Mr Greedy said,
"Now you must rest to let your stomach settle."

There was a loud THUMP!

And you know what that was, don't you?

That's right!

Little Miss Busy had fallen over backwards.

On Thursday, Mr Nonsense
popped in to see Little Miss Busy.

He brought her … an umbrella!

"Hello," he said.
"I hear you're feeling well. You don't need a rest … "

Little Miss Busy jumped for joy, right out of bed.
" … you need a holiday!" finished Mr Nonsense.

There was a loud THUMP!
That's right.
"There, you look better already," said Mr Nonsense,
and left …

… by the open window.

Little Miss Busy picked herself up.

A small smile formed on her face.

Something Mr Nonsense had said
had actually made sense.

She had never thought of going on holiday before.

The more she thought about it the happier she felt.

She thought of all the fun things she could do.

There was the planning and organising,
there was all the shopping she would have to do,
there was the packing,
and she would have to learn the language,
and read lots of books about the place she was going to.

What a lot of work!

Little Miss Busy smiled happily.

The following Thursday, she was awake at three o'clock in the morning.

Everything was ready.

Little Miss Busy had had one of the busiest weeks of her life.

Which is saying something!

She had only one thing left to do.

And that was …

... to learn how to twiddle her thumbs!

SPECIAL OFFERS FOR MR MEN AND LITTLE MISS READERS

In every Mr Men and Little Miss book you will find a special token. Collect only six tokens and we will send you a super poster of your choice featuring all your favourite Mr Men or Little Miss friends.

And for the first 4,000 readers we hear from, we will send you a Mr Men activity pad* and a bookmark* as well – absolutely free!

Return this page with six tokens from Mr Men and/or Little Miss books to:
Marketing Department, World International Limited, Deanway Technology Centre, Wilmslow Road, Handforth, Cheshire SK9 3ET.

Your name:_____

Address:_____

_____

_____ Postcode: _____

Signature of parent or guardian: _____

I enclose **six** tokens – please send me a Mr Men poster ☐
I enclose **six** tokens – please send me a Little Miss poster ☐

We may occasionally wish to advise you of other children's books that we publish. If you would rather we didn't, please tick this box ☐

*while stocks last   (Please note: this offer is limited to a maximum of two posters per household.)

Collect six of these tokens. You will find one inside every Mr Men and Little Miss book which has this special offer.

1 TOKEN

Please remove this page carefully

Join the
MR. MEN & *little miss* Club

Treat your child to membership of the long-awaited Mr Men & Little Miss Club and see their delight when they receive a personal letter from Mr Happy and Little Miss Giggles, a club badge **with their name on**, and a superb Welcome Pack. And imagine how thrilled they'll be to receive a card from the Mr Men and Little Misses on their birthday and at Christmas!

Take a look at all of the great things in the Welcome Pack, every one of them of superb quality (*see box right*). If it were

on sale in the shops, the Pack alone would cost around £12.00. But a year's membership, including all of the other Club benefits, costs just **£7.99** (plus 70p postage) with a 14 day money-back guarantee if you're not delighted.

To enrol your child please send **your** name, address and telephone number together with **your child's** full name, date of birth and address (including postcode) and a cheque or postal order for £8.69 (payable to Mr Men & Little Miss Club) to: Mr Happy, Happyland (Dept. WI), PO Box 142, Horsham RH13 5FJ. Or call 01403 242727 to pay by credit card.

Please note: We reserve the right to change the terms of this offer (including the contents of the Welcome Pack) at any time but we offer a 14 day no-quibble money-back guarantee. We do not sell directly to children - all communications (except the Welcome Pack) will be via parents/guardians. After 31/12/96 please call to check that the price is still valid. Please allow 28 days for delivery. Promoter: Robell Media Promotions Limited, registered in England number 2852153.

The Welcome Pack:

✓ Membership card
✓ Personalized badge
✓ Club members' cassette with Mr Men stories and songs
✓ Copy of Mr Men magazine
✓ Mr Men sticker book
✓ Tiny Mr Men flock figure
✓ Personal Mr Men notebook
✓ Mr Men bendy pen
✓ Mr Men eraser
✓ Mr Men book mark
✓ Mr Men key ring

Plus:

✓ Birthday card
✓ Christmas card
✓ Exclusive offers
✓ Easy way to order Mr Men & Little Miss merchandise

All for just £7.99! (plus 70p postage)